The Furry Tailed Adventures of Milady D'Ferret

and Her Acquaintances

by

Mary 'Klibs' Dralle

First Edition

All My Cats and Weasels Publishing

This Book is dedicated to my 'nieces' Jamie, Hailey, and Drew who loved to play with my ferrets . . .

And to Marie and Caelan who always asked about and thought of my little ones fondly . . .

Blessed be to all of you

In memory of Dave Bittner who wanted me to tell everyone about the benefits of ferrets . . . Dave, our world is better because you were in it

The Furry Tail Adventures of Milady D'Ferret

Table of Contents

The Furry Tail Adventures of Milady D'Ferret
Table of Contents ~ Continued

What this book is about . . .

In the winter of 2010, a wee sprite of a ferret was dropped off at an animal research facility in Ramona, California. While the staff knew how to take care of ferrets, they did not have enough time in the day to spend with her as they were involved with several environmental studies in Southern California and Montana. Their focus was the dwindling population of the Golden Eagle. Every year, this facility holds an event called Hawk Watch. It is pivotal in educating the public on the plight of raptors. One volunteer, Mary 'Klibs' Dralle (her last name rhymes with trolley), met the ferret and became her best friend. When the time came, Mary was asked to take the ferret home with her as she needed more attention than the staff could give. Other volunteers often inquired about the ferret and her adjustment to her new life and home. These are her stories . . . .

Acknowledgments . . .

To Joyce Stark, who loved all of the letters on Milady D'Ferret's Furry Tailed Adventures, encouraged the creation of this book, and sketched the story marker pencil drawings

To Dave and Leigh Bitner, who thought I would be the best person to take care of Milady

To Elizabeth Podsiadlo who, an author in her own right, kept saying, 'You can do this! Just start writing.'

To Penny Stephens, my mentor, who always stretched me to do more in my life to help others.

To Ed Seymour, Poet On The Spot™, Helen 'Marsh' Rigby, and Stacy Efrom Bart who showed me how to become a self published author

To my wonderful editors, Vicki Moen and Dana Munkelt

To Daniel Kim at Custom Embroidery in Vista, California who lovingly added each name to my Green Fleece WRI Memorial Jacket after listening to the life story of each of my ferrets before beginning his work

To Justen Kwong for giving me Shepard's picture for the opening story marker drawing coming out of a tube

To Regina Rios for giving me Rusty's picture for the closing story marker drawing sliding out of a tube on his back

Quinten York for allowing me to post his solution on keeping ferrets out of the bottom of a couch

Thank you all y'all so much for everything . . .
I love all y'all to the moon and back

Care & Feeding of a Real Weasel
By Ed Seymour
Poet On The Spot ™
Written for Mary on *November 12, 2017 at the
North San Diego (Sikes Adobe) Certified Farmers Market
Written below with permission.*

Sleep
Beauty
Rest
Is
Utmost
On
The
List.
Deprived,
They
can
become
Depraved.
Allowed
Their
Down
Time,
They
can
be
Down
right
Cuddly
or
Perhaps
Tolerant
of
People

Who
fail
To
See
Them
as
The
Fierce,
Clever,
Cunning,
Problem
solvers
they
can
become
for
a
few
choice
Hours.
then
off
they
go
for
a
micro
hibernation

New Faces, New Friends, New Life

Dear Friend,

As you have asked how I am doing,
I thought it best to send you this note . . .
My life is good and here is why . . .

Now, I had a good family but they were having
problems and sent me to live at an animal shelter.
This shelter had a lot of good people but there was always so much for
them to do that they did not have a lot of time to spend with me. Once,
there was a woman who came to visit me. She was very nice and had a
green fleece jacket that was comfortable to sleep in. She would take me
out of my cage and I loved her from the start as I would kiss her from the
moment she first held me. She was gentle and kind to me. One day, I went
to live in her castle and she is the best Serving Wench I have ever had.

In my new castle, Sundays are so special. The Serving Wench stays in the
castle all day and I get to roam the entire castle as I please. The day starts
early and I put the house cats in their place. After all, I rule this domicile!
The Serving Wench cleans my abode from top to bottom and refreshes
both of my food supplies. Although she refreshes my food and water twice
a day, Sundays allow her more time to detail her cleaning responsibilities.

Once my abode is revitalized, it is on to my personal cleaning. My coat is
brushed with at least one hundred strokes so that it will maintain its luster.
I count and let the Serving Wench know when her task is completed. Then
it is on to a pedicure, dental cleaning and ear wash. All of this is done to
keep up my appearance. After all, a Ferret must look her best in case
suitors call.

When I look my best, its play time and the Serving Wench has learned that
I like to play rough. I do not bite her anymore and I think she likes that a
lot. We play tug-o-war a lot and she tickles me until I giggle!! We have a
good time.

After all of that play time, I have a little snack from the China bowl on the coffee table and take a long nap underneath the settle. There is a good supply of blankets, towels and pillow cases. Then it is on to round two of play time and the Serving Wench who drops everything to tend to my needs. When she has done a good job, I ply her with many kisses.

It is good to be the queen!

Best Regards,

Milady D'Ferret

In my own words

Note: The title, Serving Wench, comes from Rodgers and Hammerstein's 1965 movie, Cinderella. This is, by far, my all time favorite childhood movie. To this day, the song, "In My Own Little Corner" still delights me. When the letters were crafted, it seemed to be a good title to use.

A ferret by any other name . . . would it be as clever?

Dear Friend,

A little history on ferrets . . . we ferrets (*Mustela putorius furo*) belong to the *Mustela* genus. This is a Latin derivation of the term *mus* for mouse. Animals in the Mustela genus include otters, weasels, polecats, stoats, black-footed ferrets, martens, badgers, wolverines, and other "mouse catchers". *Putorius* is from the Latin *putor*, which means a stench referring to our musky odor. Furo comes from the Latin *furonem* meaning "thief". So we have a "mouse-catching, smelly, thief"! The word ferret most likely comes from the Latin *furo* or the Italian *furone* with the same meaning of "thief".

As some of you may know, I have chosen to change my name. My former caretakers called me Patron Tequila. Now I ask you, does that sound like a name for a ferret of my caliber? I should think not! My new Serving Wench decided to call me Milady D'Ferret. Translated, it means My Lady of Ferrets. It comes from a book, the Three Musketeers, by Alexander Dumas. In the back of the book, there was a character, Milady D'Winter. She was the criminal wife of Athos, one of the Three Musketeers. In the story Mr. Dumas told of a woman who was forced into the convent as a teenager. She fell in love with a priest and they fled the church with stolen property. Because they were thieves, they were branded.

Although I am not a thief, as my genus states, I am considered a criminal in California because of a 1939 law that says we are bad animals and might interfere with the wildlife if we escape. There was a long story, written in 2010, by G.O. Graening that proves we have not started any big colonies of ferrets here in the United States. Oh sure, some people think that they can let us loose and we will be able to take care of ourselves. That is not true. Often times, we will walk up to someone in hopes that they will take care of us. Many of us starve to death as we need to eat meat every four hours because of our high metabolic rate. And we do not know how to hunt anymore because we are very dependent on humans.

Now, some of us can be quite useful. Did you know that if I lived in New York City with a couple of Harris's Hawk and a rat terrier, my Serving Wench could go into business as a Natural Vermin Exterminator? It is because of our ability to hunt and eat vermin that we were domesticated in the first place all those many years ago.

Also, I have a brand of sorts . . . a tattoo in my right ear, two dots, which means that I have been spayed and de-scented. Thus the new name, Milady D'Ferret!

Best Regards,

Milady D'Ferret

In my own words

Note: Little did I know that when I brought Milady home, she was deaf. While she was at the research facility, she bit everyone who tried to hold her. Except me. She would bite because she was frightened. Something about my energy let her know, I was a little different. Maybe she could sense that I am an Earth Mother and Witch with a good connection to animals.

Hold you me!

Dear Friend,

One of you wanted to know how the Serving Wench catches me if I am not wearing that awful harness. You see, after I get done surveying the castle, I seek out my Serving Wench, climb on top of her foot and lift up my right front paw to signal her to pick me up. Well, here is what she does, she lets her breath out, bends over, takes a breath in and and picks me up. She said she learned the breathing technique in yogurt. Or was that yoga?

Now, she has a special way of holding me. Her palm is always up and my front paws are centered on it. Then she bends her arm next to her body and I snuggle in close to her. When I am comfortable and feel secure, I give her a kiss. She tries so hard.

Sometimes, other creatures, like my Serving Wench, come to our castle and if I do not like them, I bite them so they know to leave me alone. I will only climb on top of my Serving Wench's foot and have her hold me. I am funny this way. That is why she took me to her castle. I mean, no one else was in tune to my needs as she was when I was at that other place.

Best Regards,

Milady D'Ferret

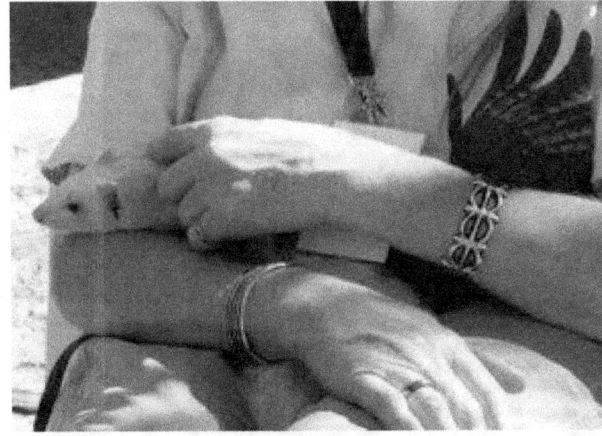

 *In my own words* While 'Hold you me!' is not grammaricly correct, it comes from a child whom I used to care for many moons ago. When she was learning to talk, she would often mix up the common phrases we use to express ourselves. This was one such phrase

Home Is Where The Heart Is . . .

Dear Friend,

   I am truly blessed to have been given my current Serving Wench. She was able to procure my former large three story abode and brought it in one day. She did not like the Fang Shui of the domicile and set to change the flow of energy. First, she removed all of the old smelly carpet pads and replaced them with new blue ones, after all, color blue belongs to the Water Fang Shui element. This color is excellent for use in the Fang Shui areas of the East for Health & Family. My health is very important and the friendship I share with my wench is turning into a familial one. After she replaced the carpet, she put cedar sawdust into some old nylons to deter any bugs from blemishing my skin. There might be another reason regarding the smell in the air but I do not pay attention to such matters. Then she gave me all new sheets, towels and blankets.

To further improve the fang shui, she removed the multiple feeder and water dishes. They were sorted and the good ones kept and cleaned. These were placed in the utmost top level of my castle. This is my bedroom. Now, I can have breakfast in bed all day long!

She removed all of the old torn toys and hammock from my large cage and put in new ones. The hammock was put into my new bedroom and the toys moved to the second level which is my romper room!! I have my carpeted tunnel toy, my beloved lady bug bag, in case I get really tired from playing, and all of the other new toys. It is wonderful.

The lower level of my castle is now the Privy. It has linoleum flooring that is easy to clean and my commode is secured in the corner so that it does not tip over on me when I use it. She mentioned that she would be able to keep it cleaner for me than when it was up on the top floor.

She found a ladder that was secured on the top of my smaller portable abode that I had been staying in. Then she attached it just below the threshold of the door on the first floor of the large cage.
It is about two inches off the ground
and I can get in by myself.

She propped open the door on the first floor of the large cage with a carabiner clip. Now, I am able to come and go as I please. The doors on the second and third floor were locked shut so that I do not fall out and hurt myself. She is so very thoughtful in the design.

We ferrets love to climb up to the top of anything! I climbed up the face of my abode and jumped off the top. It is really tall and it was not a graceful moment. In the days that followed, my Serving Wench got a long black tube. She put it on end on the top of my abode and wrapped it all of the way around to the ground securing it with cable ties in several places. So, I would climb up the tube and spend time at the top. Then, I would slide down and come out giggling! It is fun.

One day, my beloved wench, brought home a new tub. She drilled holes into the bottom and secured it to the top of my abode with cable ties. She put a carpet mat in the bottom of the tub and some towels, blankets, and pillow cases. My abode now had a penthouse flat. She is so marvelously kind. She got a lot of kisses that night . . .

I was so happy to be in my newly renovated abode all day, I did not leave it for my favorite place in the castle, under the settle!

My life is good and I am so fortunate to have this Serving Wench. I hope our friendship lasts a long time.

Ta Ta For Now,

Milady D'Ferret

In my own words

Note: The name of the cage or abode was changed to the Kriminal's Kondo in later stories

How to install a Penthouse Access Tube:

In my own words

The drain tube, 90 degree elbow, and zip ties were procured from Lowes. Pool noodle, used as padding, was found at Walmart. Total cost was under $20.00 at the time .

Drain tube was washed in the bath tub with soap and hot water. It was left to dry outside for about a week to eliminate any soil and/or noxious fumes.

Starting at the top, a 90 degree elbow was used and pushed it on the end of the drain tube. This keeps the ferret from falling off the top when trying to find the entrance. (Part of the pool noodle was removed in the very front of the photo to show elbow better)

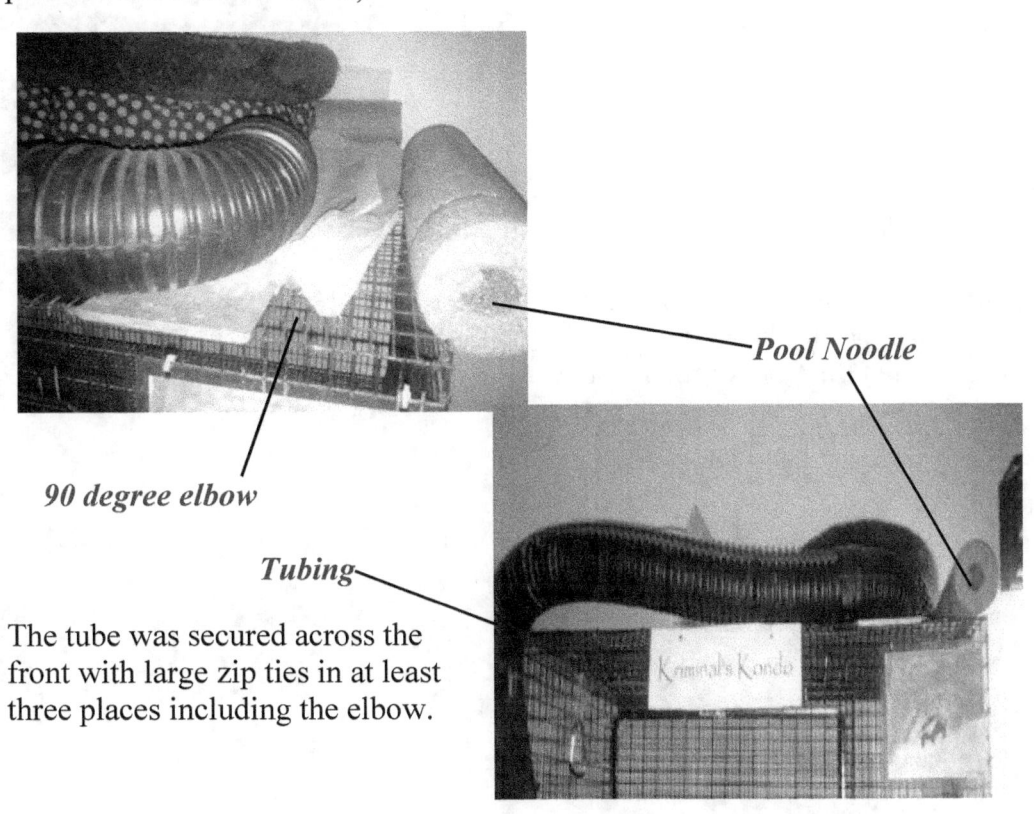

Pool Noodle

90 degree elbow

Tubing

The tube was secured across the front with large zip ties in at least three places including the elbow.

Wrap the tube around the side of the Kondo in a gradual slope to the floor. Secure with large zip ties in at least four places

.

Allow at least a two foot contact with the floor back behind the Kondo. It is better that the exit is behind the Kondo as it keeps the ferrets from being underfoot at the front of the Kondo.

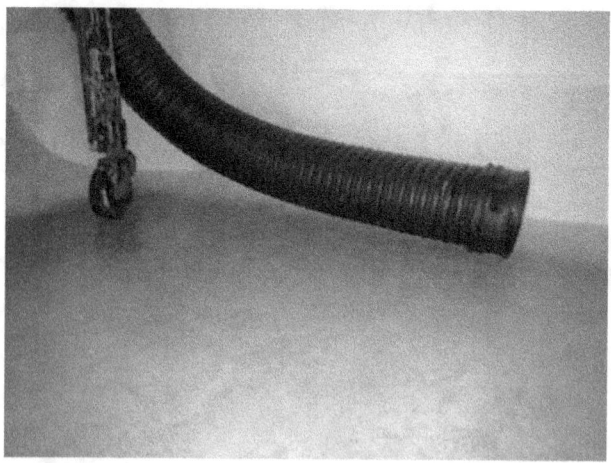

The Necessities of Life are Water, Shelter & Food

Food, glorious food!
We're anxious to try it
Three banquets a day --
Our favorite diet!
From Oliver
Written by: Lionel Bart

Dear Friend,

We ferrets have special dietary needs. In the wild, we eat very high protein meals and need to have a lot of taurine, an essential amino acid found in meat. We love meat. Lots of meat and we like it raw. Truth be told, all animals do better on a diet of raw food. Just plain raw meat.

Ferrets, like me, are originally from Europe. In Europe, we eat rodents like mice, moles, voles, rabbits and such. When we get desperate, we will eat bugs but they are not that satisfying.

As I am domesticated, I do not have to find my own food, thank goodness. It is provided in small bowls strategically placed in our castle. One, as mentioned before, is on the top level of my abode. The other, also mentioned before, is on the coffee table.

However, it is easier for humans to buy cooked food that will be good for a long time. Some of the 'stuff' that is put into the canned food is not good for us either. I had always had a diet of cooked meat and really like it. So, I do not eat raw meat but I do love raw eggs!

Our cousins here in North America, the Black Footed Ferret, diet consists of Prairie Dogs. When the Prairie Dog population plummeted because of distemper and man's encroachment, so did the ferret population. Thankfully, some took action and now there are a lot more Black Footed Ferrets and they are still endangered.

Bon Appétit,
Milady D'Ferret

The Chase Is On!

Dear Friend,

It is an early summer night here with so much light in the evening and the Serving Wench likes to play my favorite game, Chase! She tries to run away from me but I can out run her with my four legs. We go thorough out the entire castle for a couple of rounds and I get so excited that I do the weasel war dance!! I spring and hop all around because we have so much fun. When we are done, we cuddle on the settle and I eat from my China bowls on the coffee table. All of that running makes me really hungry. After awhile, it is time for a nap under my favorite summer time place in the castle, the settle.

Some of you may wonder what I mean by the settle. The Serving Wench has a wooden sofa that is called a Settle in the Arts and Crafts Movement of the 1890's. She had seen one on a tour of the Gamble House in Pasadena and bought one for herself when it came time for new furniture. It is better than a traditional couch/sofa as we cannot get caught inside and the cats cannot claw the corners to tear the fabric. Some people call them futons. It is such a special space and the cats respect it. I have wonderful blankets, flannel sheets, a pillow case, and soft towel so that I can nap in total comfort.

Best Regards,
Milady D'Ferret

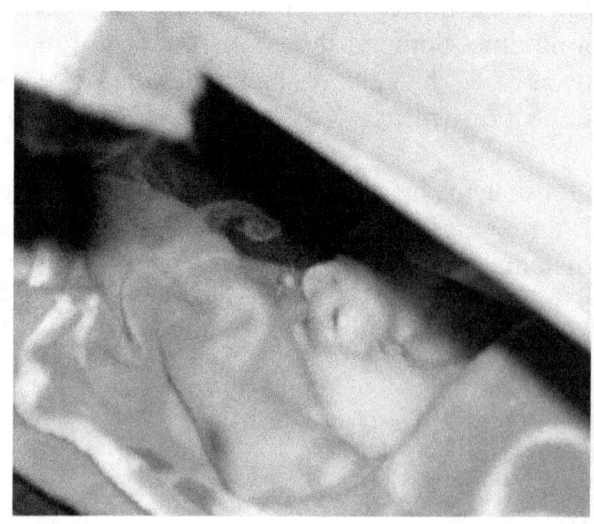

Nothing like a nice relaxing bath

Dear Friend,

I have been a little itchy of late. It must be this summer heat. My Serving Wench saw that I was just plain miserable. She left me in the living room as she went out to the kitchen. She took something out of the pantry and then found a large white high walled plastic container. Mind you, I had to chase her through the house to see her do all of this and we wound up in the bathroom. She started the water as I could smell it. I tried to get into the tub but the walls were too slippery and I slid down to the floor. Then she opened the container from the pantry and poured something from it into the water. After a little bit, she picked me up and put me into the wonderful water. It was not like the drinking water in my bowl that is cool and refreshing. This water was warm and had texture. She started to rub me all over with her hands. What ever that stuff was from the pantry container really felt soft and soothing on my skin. She must have left me in there for a long time. After a while, she ran some more warm water to rinse me off and wrapped me in a clean warm towel. Oh, this was most delightful and I rolled in that towel for a very long time. I hope we do it again and soon!

Best Regards,

Milady D'Ferret

In my own words **Ferret Care Note:** When ferret's skin gets dry, an oatmeal bath is just the thing to make them feel better.
Add 1 cup of oatmeal to a blender and run on high until it is a fine powder. The brand does not matter and it must be plain without any flavors, sugar or other common oatmeal ingredients.
Fill a dish tub or large bucket with warm -- but not hot -- water, 70 to 80° F (21 to 27° C) is ideal. If you are bathing your ferret outside in the summer, lower temperatures are fine. Pour the crushed oatmeal into the tub and stir with a large spoon or stick.

Place your ferret in the tub and allow them to soak for five to ten minutes. If your ferret won't sit still in the tub, hold them and pour the oatmeal mix onto their fur coat and skin, gently rubbing it in.

Rinse your ferret and then towel-dry them. Brush them out with a brush appropriate for their fur coat while they are drying.

Things That Go Bump In The Night

Dear Friends,

It is the month of August and called the Dog Days because if you look up in the night sky, you can see the constellation Sirius, the Dog Star, from about July 22nd to August 22nd! This time of the year is very hot and can be hard on us animals. When the Serving Wench comes home to the castle, she opens up the windows and puts a fan in them to help circulate the air. We are very fortunate; our front door has a metal security screen door. This really helps cool down the front of the castle. The Serving Wench lets me stay out of my abode and sleep under the settle all night long.

Also, to help cool me off, she wraps frozen water bottles with wash cloths and places them in my bed under the settle. Then, depending on the heat of the day, I lay across them and become comfortably cool.

In the night, my Serving Wench sleeps on top of the settle. This is great because I can crawl up on top of her, ply her with kisses as I am so happy to be able to sleep in my favorite space with her. Then I get a little something to drink, go to the bathroom in my living room commode and go back to sleep. Sometimes, I make a bit of noise and things go bump in the night. What a wonderful life . . . I am happy.

Happily,

Milady D'Ferret

This Is The Way We Wash Our Clothes . . .

Dear Friend,

Early one morning, when I came back to my abode after a morning outing in the castle, my favorite blankets were gone. In their place was one not-so-soft pillow case and rough towel. I was upset . . . what had I done wrong . . . why was I being punished??? I spent the day contemplating my actions . . . why had the Serving Wench done this to me . . .

The Serving Wench was gone for such a long time that day and late into the night. Where was she? What was she doing? Why was she not tending to my needs? Finally, she came back to the castle. She opened my abode and took me out. We went to the living room just like any other night but something was different. All of my blankets and such, under the settle, smelled wonderful and were amazingly soft. Later that night, she put me back into my abode and all of my blankets were there. They smelled wonderful and were amazingly soft, too. She had taken all of my items and cleaned them. She did it out of love. I was so comfortable that I slept all night long and halfway into the next morning. When I finally got up, I plied the Serving Wench with a lot of kisses. She is such a good caregiver!

Best Regards,

Milady D'Ferret

Ferrets in Art

Dear Friend,

Believe it or not, there have been quite a few ferrets in the art world. There are two shown below. The one on the left was painted by one of the most famous of painters, Leonardo da Vinci, "Lady with Ermine" between 1489-1491. It was done for Duke Ludovico Sforza of Milan. He was a very powerful merchant in Renaissance Italy. Cecilia Gallerani is the woman and a lady-in-waiting who became the duke's mistress. The ermine she holds, a stoat (Mustela erminea), in its winter coat, is a highly valued creature, and here it provides the key to understanding the multiple layers of meaning conveyed by the portrait. The Greek word for the animal is galee, a play on the word "Gallerani" which was Cecilia's family name. The ermine also refers to her character: according to legend, the ermine is too fastidious to dirty its fur and refers to Cecilia's wholesome or pure nature. It is important that the ermine also refers directly to Duke Ludovico himself. Having received the insignia of the chivalric Order of the Ermine from the King of Naples in 1488, Ludovico was nicknamed Italico Morel bianco ermellino ("Italian Moor, white ermine"). Thus the painting celebrates both the girl's beauty and the couples' relationship. As based on the article found at https://www.wisdomportal.com/Stanford/LadyWithAnErmine.html for the exhibit in tth Legion of Honor at the the Fine Arts Museums of San Francisco, May 13, 2003.

This is a painting by Leonardo da Vinci, his "Lady with Ermine."

This is a photograph by Joyce Stark, her "Volunteer with Ferret."

A Long Cool Ferret in a Black Tube

Dear Friend,

In nature, as you may know, we ferrets live underground just like with our prey. We like being down in our tunnels as Our Mother, The Earth's soil temperature is in the upper sixties. We have a hard time when it is hot. When you live in a castle like mine, having an underground tunnel is not possible. My Serving Wench more bought black flexible drain pipe. It is about six inches in diameter and ten feet long. She put it behind the settle and I love it. I run in and out of it all of the time. One night though, I scared my Serving Wench. You see, my backside was very itchy and I turned myself over so that I could itch. Using my paws on the top of the pipe, I would itch and rub my back. The sound alarmed her as I would start and stop in the entire ten feet. When she saw me come out on my back side she was so relieved and understood what I had done.

As she mentioned earlier, in the story, How to install a Penthouse Access Tube, she bought another length of pipe and, starting at the top of my three story abode, she secured it with cable ties and wrapped it around the abode and down to the ground. Well, I tell you, this was wonderful. I no longer had to climb up the face of my abode to get to the top. I could crawl up and slide down my pipe. It was great fun. Then, she did something else, she secured a plastic box to the top and filled it with a collection of blankets and sheets. My abode now had a penthouse flat. She is so marvelously kind.

Best Regards,

Milady D'Ferret

Harry Potter Festival

Dear Friend,

My Serving Wench loves to read good books that show a great creative story. And so it was with J.K. Rowling's Harry Potter series of books. She read them all long before the movies came out. And then, she bought all of the movies

One day, she decided to have a Harry Potter movie marathon. She had a great many of the items in her home as well. She dressed up my long black drain pipes as Nagini, Lord Voldemort's pet snake and loyal servant. Those pipes made great snake decorations! And then she set about with the rest of the decorations:

Candles/Soft Lights
Purple Bedsheet Over Coffee Table/Light Under Coffee Table
Professor Mcgonagall Outfit – Purple Dress/Black Jacket/Purple/Reading Glasses
Errol, The Owl
Hogwart's School Of Witchcraft And Wizardry Letter
Harry Potter's Glasses
Nimbus 2000 that her brother, Mike, made for her one birthday
Sorting Hat
Luna Lovegood's Wand
Black Cauldron With Assorted Chocolates
Sorcerer's Stone
Tom Riddle's Diary W/Raven Feather Quill
Tom Riddle's Mother's Ring
A bottle of Polly Juice Potion
Crookshank (as portrayed by Riley, her orange cat)
The ferret that was put down Draco's pant leg (as portrayed by me, Miladay)
Crystal Ball
Tea Cups & Pot
A Dementor

Whomping Willow (as portrayed by Benny, The Ficus Benjamina)
Pensive & Little Bottles Of Memories
Marauder's Map
Fife
Stone Runes with a Maroon Casting Cloth
Resurrection Stone
Cloak of Invisibility
Over Sized Spider
Nagini (Oversized Snake-Drain Pipe w/Felt Head & Tail)
Prophecy Orb on a holder
Rat
Leprechauns's Gold Coins
Book of Spells – Herbal Medicine, Celtic Magic, Druid Magic and Dragons
Guests's Names on Burnt Paper next to the cauldron

Not only did she decorate the house, she made the most wonderful foods to share with me and her guests. Well, the guest had far more of the foods she made than I did. And the fool smelled wonderful.

Breakfast was served at 10:00 a.m. Pumpkin Pecan Waffles served with Chai Tea
Lunch followed at 12: 00 p.m. Brie and Cranberry Port Sauce served with New Mexico Dry Rub Pecans and Fresh Baked Bread
A Light Snack was offered at 2:00 p.m. Crab Cakes served with Wicked Wine
At about 6:30 p.m., it was time for Dinner
Dill Salmon
Garlicky Mashed Potatoes
Lemony Green Beans
Sautéed Greens
Salad made of Greens, sliced Green Onions, diced Bell Peppers, Sunflower Seeds, Peas, White Beans and Shaved Parmesan Cheese. With a light dressing of Champagne Vinegar and Grape Seed Oil
For drinks, Pumpkin Ale or Lime Sparkling Water, were provided
Dessert at 8:30 p.m. Cherry Pie With Vanilla Ice Cream

It was a fun filled day for all who attended.

Cancer Victory Saddened by the passing of Milady D'Ferret

In my own words Hello Friend,

As some of you already know, the surgery on May 15, 2012 was a complete success. The events of the day were a blessing from the start and when Barbara Gensler checked on me before the start of the surgery, it settled my spirit as she is now the Head Charge Nurse and hand picked the nurses on my team. Dr. Worsey successfully removed the entire tumor, part of my colon, and lymph nodes. He took pictures of the event and shared them with Mike, my little brother, and Jacquee, my best friend of 35 years, while I was in recovery. Jacquee was very interested in the pictures while Mike was subdued! On Thursday morning, I was given communion by a Eucharistic minister from the Catholic Church. It was a blessing. Shortly after receiving communion, Dr. Worsey came into tell me that the tumor was stage 1 and the nodes were all clear. This means no Chemo but still means I have check ups every three months for the next year. This is not a problem! He released me from the hospital on Friday and Jacquee drove me home. It reminded me of the old days when we would come north up the Interstate 5 from many our adventures in San Diego!

This victory was short lived however, as an hour and half after I arrived home, my beloved Milady D'Ferret suffered a seizure brought on by Insulinoma. This is a cancer of the pancreatic beta (insulin producing) cells. Although I took her to the vet, it was not possible to save her. She was too far gone. I had to make a tough decision and put her to sleep. As my green fleece WRI jacket was the way we met, I thought it only fitting that it should be used when we parted. I did not know that the she had this condition. Her vet told me that they hide this well and when it hits, it is hard. He was amazed to find out that I had adopted an older, illegal animal. As part of her memorial, her name was place on to my Green Fleece WRI Memorial Jacket that she loved to sleep in with the words, In Loving Memory of Milady D'Ferret ? - 5/16/12.

Much love, prayer and gratitude,

Mary 'Klibs' Dralle

If it should be . . .

If it should be that I grow weak
And pain should keep me from my sleep;
Then you must do what must be done,
For this last battle can't be won.

You will be sad, I understand;
But don't let grief then stay your hand.
For this day more than all the rest,
Your love for me must stand the test.

We've had so many happy years;
What is to come can hold no fears.
You don't want me to suffer so
The time has come, please let me go.

Take me where my needs they'll tend,
But please stay with me 'til the end
To hold me close and speak to me
Until my eyes no longer see.

I know in time you will agree,
It was a kindness done for me.
Although my tail its last has waved,
From pain and suffering I'm saved.

Please do not grieve that it was you
Who had this painful thing to do.
We've been so close, we two, these years;
Don't let your heart hold any tears.

Author Unknown

Her Acquaintances

as defined in
https://dictionary.cambridge.org/us/dictionary/English/
acquaintance - a person whom you know but do not know
well and who is therefore not exactly a friend

All of these Ferrets were welcomed into my home after Milady
had passed. While she never met them, my care of them was
inspired by her.

Here are their stories in order of entry to my home:

Mundungus - A Cinnamon Sable Boy

LuLu - A Dark Eyed White Girl

Tazz - A Chocolate Sable Boy

Summer Time ... Fun Time
My Hidey Hole
Now Tazz!
Two Little Girls Come A Calling
The Gate
Summer of 2015
Ultimate Pet Fountain for my Health
Tazz's Tribute, Sept 14, 2016

Rascal - A Charcoal Sable Girl

Rufia - A Dark Eyed White Girl

Bonnie - A Chocolate Sable Girl

My First Little Boo-boo
Bonnie's Second Little Boo-boo

Dylan - A Dark Eyed White Boy

Her Acquaintance

Mundungus – A Cinnamon Sable Boy

Hello Friend,

My name is Mundungus Ferret, at your service. On or about June 14th, aka Flag Day, I came to live with Mary and her cats. A ferret rescue group had called her to see if she would take me in. She said yes and drove a long way to come get me. She loved me at first sight because of my luscious Cinnamon Sable fur. She did not know my real name and gave the name of a thief in the Harry Potter books, Mundungus Fletcher. She was my new Momma and that is what I choose to call her.

When we got home, I had to go to the bathroom right away. When Momma saw what came out, she got a little sad, picked me up and kissed me. You see, my poop was green and she knew that I was a sick little boy. On her Ferret Poop Chart, this is what it said,

'Green Ferret Poop: A very non-specific sign — it just means that food is moving through too fast. The normal brown color seen in feces is the end product of break down of old red blood cells. The pigment goes through a green stage called biliverdin before it becomes brown (called stercobilin). So if it goes through at an accelerated rate, it never breaks down all the way and has a green color to it. Anything that accelerates passage of food or causes diarrhea can result in green color — ECE, rapid food changes, lymphoma, just about anything.'

From The Ferret Poop Chart - A guide to what different types of poop might indicate about a ferret's health. By Bruce H. Williams, DVM, DACVP

The next day, she made an appointment and took me to see a nice woman. I could sense that she was a bit upset after she told me how Milady had passed was in May of 2012.

Momma took me to see a very nice woman who stuck me with a needle and took some blood for testing. We went back home and I had a bit to eat and started to play with Riley, Momma's orange tabby cat. He was a lot of fun but I got tired pretty quickly. I put my self to bed in the Kriminal's Kondo and slept until the next morning. I was really tired.

A couple of days later, the nice woman called Momma to say that I had a liver problem. Momma left and came back with some not so tasty liquids for me to take a couple of times a day. They did not taste so good and I took them anyway.

Every day was good because Riley and I would play a lot. He was a really neat cat and I liked him tons! One night, I did not want to play with Riley and he started talking to Momma. She told me that she would be taking me to see the nice woman the next day. I thought that would be fun.

The next morning, I felt awful. Momma got into the shower to get ready to take me to my visit. Something happened and I felt drawn to this beautiful place. I will describe it to you ... There were meadows and hills where I could run and play together with my litter mates ...there was plenty of food, water and sunshine so that I was warm and comfortable ... I felt restored to health and vigor all the while being whole and strong again ... It was a great place for me to be and I said goodbye to Riley.

He let out a very loud meow and Momma came in the bedroom. She looked at Riley who looked at the Kriminal's Kondo and meowed again. She let out an ear-splitting, "NO!" as she understood what Riley was telling her. I saw her pick up my still body and gently kiss me with a tear filled eye. She was so sad that I left. She called the nice woman to cancel my appointment and when they asked why she cried real hard and said I had died.

She added my name to the Green Fleece WRI Memorial Jacket and did not think she would ever take in another ferret

All my love and kisses,
Mundungus Ferret

Mundungus Ferret peeking out from
under the closet door.

Riley regally sitting atop the television
surveying his domain

Her Acquaintance
LuLu - A Dark Eyed White Girl

Hello Friend,

In July of 2012, a man named Pat Wright, from Legalize Ferrets, called Mary and asked her to provide foster care for me, LuLu, and my bonded mate, Tazz. Now, I was a little older, about 6 or so, than Tazz, who was about 2 at the time. Mary brought in her own carrier and when one of Pat's dogs jump on Mary, she used her Rottweiler training voice. It was a very low octave and she said a big, NO! The dog did not jump on her ever again. I could tell that she had been around animals.

Pat lovingly handed me over to her and then went about finding Tazz. He was playing hide and seek with one of the other weasels. Let me tell you, that ferret was a huge handful. I mean that figuratively and literally. He had so much energy and weighed a whopping 2.5 lbs. Mary held both of us in her arms and Pat took her picture. He wanted to send it to our owner.

We left and were on our way to a new home with the promise of fun and adventure. Boy, was it adventure. We had never lived with cats before and Mary had five of them - Rascal, Ransom, Remy, Raven and Riley. I was not too crazy about cats but Tazz and Riley became really good friends. I liked that as I liked to sleep a lot. Those two would spend a long time playing chase. And they took turns. It usually stared with Riley chasing Tazz, then Tazz chasing Riley then Riley chasing Tazz and so on for hours at a time. It really was very comical.

Mary let us free roam all around her home. That was so nice. Well, I take that back a bit as there was one room, her office, that we were not allowed into. She had a lot of stuff in there that could harm us. The other ferrets did not go into that room at all either because she had a piece of plywood that blocked the entrance. She kept talking about making a picket fence gate but did not get it built in my time with her.

Mary took good care of Tazz and me. She would come home from work, pick us up, cuddle us, feed us and clean up after us. Life with her was just wonderful except for the summer time. It gets really, really hot in her home. She would put box fans in the windows of our home. We really liked the one in the master bedroom because it blew across the bed. She had stairs at the foot of the bed and we could climb up on it and sit right in front of the fan. In the living room, she would leave the front door open all night as she had a security screen door with a dead bolt. Tazz and I could sleep on the threshold all night long. It was divine.

Every now and again, Mary would take us to visit this nice woman. She would feel us all over and thought that Tazz was a spaz that everyone in her office just loved! One gal could hardly wait for Mary to take him out of our crate. She would give me a 'shot' of something called, DeLorean. At least that is what I heard. It would hurt and Mary would get a bit worried about me. The nice woman said it would help with my insulinoma ... Whatever that meant. The shot hurt a lot. When I would come home, I would sleep for a long time and was grumpy with Tazz. After a couple of days, I felt all better.

Life with Mary was very loving. The longer we stayed with her, the slower I was moving. I was getting a bit older. One day, she left for work and I looked all over the house for her and finally laid down by the door in the laundry room. She used it to go in and out of the house. Something happened and I felt drawn to this beautiful place. I will describe it to you ... There were meadows and hills where I could run and play together with my litter mates ...there was plenty of food, water and sunshine so that I was warm and comfortable ... I felt restored to health and vigor all the while being whole and strong again ... It was a great place for me to be ... I decided to go there and left Mary. She found my body when she came home and buried my in her yard. She cried a lot and Tazz kissed her, too.

Now, he was the only ferret in the house. A couple of weeks later, she put my name on the Green Fleece WRI Memorial Jacket , . . Lovely LuLu . . . How marvelously kind.

Lovingly,
LuLu

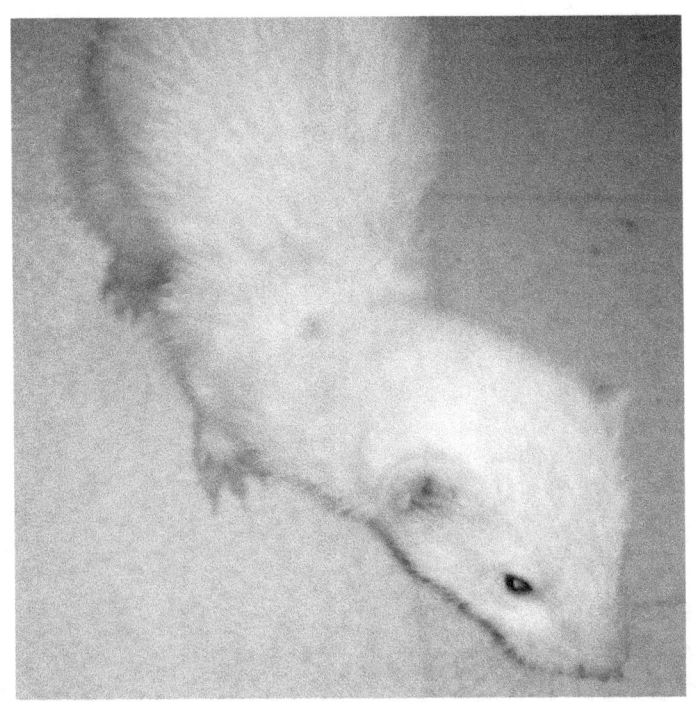

Lovely LuLu . . .

Her Acquaintance
Tazz, A Chocolate Sable Boy

Hello Friend,

As she described in her story, LuLu and I arrived here in July of 2012. Now, I just loved my wife, LuLu. She was a very pretty dark eyed white sprite. She was a bit older than me and reminded Mary of the lyrics in the song "Edge of Seventeen" by Stevie Nicks. While the song was really about the passing of her uncle and John Lennon in 1980, the part where she sings about how young he was and did not seem happy, made her love him all the more. LuLu would look at me like that sometimes. I really did love her.

Anyway, I digress. We liked living here with Mary and her cats. They were mostly okay except for one named Raven. His elevator did not go all the way up, if you know what I mean. He made a lot of work for Mary as she had to clean up after him all of the time and in so many ways. We had never been around cats and they were proving to be a lot of fun. Especially, Riley, the Orange Tabby Cat. He told me that he was born in a shelter on Halloween 2005 and was adopted by one of Mary's neighbors. They let him out one day, June 14th, 2006, Flag Day. He remembered that day as he was from the Camp Pendleton Marine Corp base and knew all of the patriotic dates! Mary brought him into the house when she came home from work the next day because he was playing in the middle of the street with Tiggy. Tiggy was another of Mary's cats but he lived outside and never wanted to be in the house. When she drove up, Tiggy got out of the street but Riley just looked at her while standing there.

Mary thought he did not have a home and a cat who did not know that cars were dangerous needed protection. She brought him in her home much to the disdain and objection of Rascal, the 18 pound furry gray barn cat from Minnesota. She put him in the office away from the other cats and took care of him. A day or two later, she let him out after Rascal settled down. It was going okay.

47

After about a week, and as no one had asked about him, she took him to the cat doctor. Come to find out, he was from the house up the street and Mary tried to return him. He did not like that house and when Mary came home, he was waiting for her on her porch door step so he moved right in! The neighbors never asked about him and he has been here ever since.

He was so much fun to play with and we did a lot together when LuLu wanted to sleep. We would run around the house making a big ruckus! Our favorite game was chase. I would chase him, then he would chase me and then I would chase him again. It was great fun and made Mary laugh to hear us running around the house.

Oh, and we would play soccer, too. Mary had these wiffle balls in golf ball and baseball sizes. Riley was really good at hitting them so that they would go flying and bouncing all over. I would chase after them and hit them, too, but I could never make them fly like Riley did. It was the best game ever. Often times, we would hear Mary laughing out loud at our shenanigans. We ferrets are a lot of serious fun.

Another thrilling game was Fling the Ferret. Mary and I would play it. First, she would get all of the pillows from around the house, pile them up in the middle of the bed and standing at the foot of the bed, gently toss me into the middle of the pillows. I would come running out of it and she would do it again and again. Sometimes, I was so very happy that I would do the Weasel War Dance right off the bed. If you want to see a ferret doing that dance, you can look for Weasel War Ferret on YouTube.

See ya,
Tazz

In my own words **Note**: This game is to be done *gently* into a lot of pillow. Never play this game with intended harm. Make sure that your ferret does not get hurt in any way and does not incur an injury.

Summer Time ... Fun Time

Well, hello again,

About those wiffle balls. Sometimes, when there was a lot of sunlight and the days were really, really hot, Mary would make a special place for me to play in the bathtub. She called it bobbing for wiffle balls. She would take a small tote, fill it part way with water and I would play bobbing for whiffle balls. I would look at the ball, put my face in the water with my eyes closed, get the ball in my mouth, take it out of the tote and set it aside. When Mary and I played the game together, there were always a lot of balls. When I would get into the tub by myself, there were only a couple of balls. I am not sure why she would take some out when I was alone. Maybe she was worried that I would hurt myself or something like that.

Speaking of summer time and hot days, in the wild, we ferrets like to live in ground as Milady had mentioned. Often, we lived in the burrows of our former prey, like rabbits. It is wonderfully cool in the earth as it stays somewhere between 50 and 60 degrees year round. My ancestors and wild relations only hunt at dawn and dusk because when it is really hot it hard being in the heat. While a burrow is not possible in Mary's home, I did manage to find some great cool places to be in.

Her dressing closet was my favorite place to be. It had a cool floor to lay on in the summer. And I knew how to climb up and get on the racks very quickly. Except for this one time. There was this tall box that I looked down into from the first rack and fell into it. Mary was gone to work for the day. Lucky for me, she found me on her lunch break and got me out. She put me on the top level of my Kriminal's Kondo with two frozen water bottles. She put them into this shape, \ /, and I loved it. I put an armpit over each one and rested my head on one, too. Talk about cool down. I must have slept all afternoon, I was so comfortable! After that, Mary would make sure that boxes like that were not out and that I always had two frozen water bottles in the Kondo.

Tootles, Tazz

In my own words **Note:** Actually, about bobbing for whffle balls, I had always put about 5 or 6 balls into the tote at a time. When Tazz would take one out, I would put it back into the tote when he was fishing out the next one, ferrets are so silly! It was his very favorite game!!!

49

My Hidey Hole

Howdy,

My fondest memory was when Mary came back from Adelanto, California in early spring of 2013 after testing the crash cushion she designed. I loved the smell of her shoes . . . and I mean LOVE. There were so many really good smells, brake dust, tire rubber, different liquids that came out of the vehicle that was tested, the soil from the facility and so much more. I just had to have this shoe all to myself as per the first of the Ferret Property Laws, If *I* like it, it is *MINE*. During the night, I took one of those shoes and dragged it under her bed . . . fyi, she has a double sided Captain's bed with four baffles in the middle to properly align the bottom drawers. I am such a little fart and managed to move three of the baffles ever so lightly so that I could get the shoe into the location behind the front baffle. I made her very late for work the next day. On the weekend, she had to take the bed apart to get the shoe. Unfortunately, she found all of the other items I stole and hid away in my stash. . . She managed to adjust the baffles so that I could not get in there anymore. To this day, she still needs to properly align the baffles but that will take help as her headboard is very, very heavy.

Signed,
Tazz (and I am Still Pissed Off)

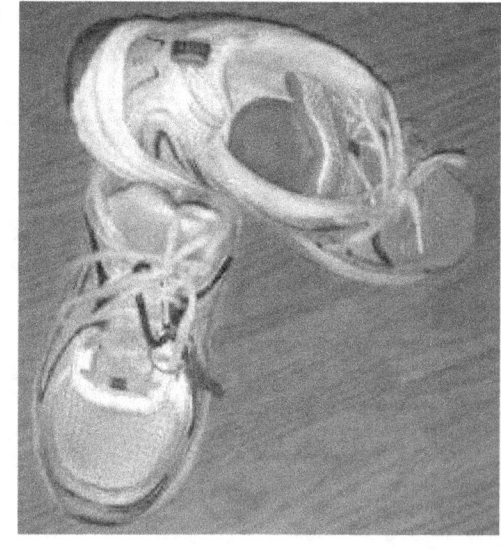

Now Tazz!

Greetings Friend,

One very sad day, my wife died. I was inconsolable for the longest time. I did not want to play with Riley nor dance my favorite powwow dance around the kitchen island. Mary did not know what to do as I was so lonely and heartbroken. So, she decided to bring in two new sprites for me. One, was a cute little charcoal gray girl named Rascal and I played with her right away. The other one, was a dark eyed white sprite named Rufia but I did not like her from the start. When I got done playing with Rascal, I found Rufia and tried to hurt her by fighting with her. Well, that cute little charcoal sprite, Rascal, did not like that one bit and started to fight with me. Next thing I know, I was stuck in the Kondo all night long. And that made me very mad. We started Kondo rotation after that incident for quite a long while. They would be in the Kondo for part of the day and I would be out and about or vice versa. No more free roaming.

After awhile, I stopped attacking Rufia but I never did warm up to her. Mary thought that a sign on our Kondo, based on a picture that someone had sent to her, would make me understand. It was of this man name Jesus. He was holding a charcoal ferret in his right hand, had a dark eyed white ferret at his feet and was scruffing a chocolate sable in his left hand. It was called "Play For You Jesus" and created by Art by Stef*. Mary printed it out and wrote, 'Now Tazz, you need to get along with Rascal and Rufia . . . it makes for a loving house", Jesus said lovingly. She hung it on the outside of our Kondo.

Later on, in this book, Mary will share Rascal and Rufia's sides of this story. I just need to tell you from my point of view.

Talk to you later,
Tazz

In my own words **Note:** Out of respect to *Stephanie Jamison and the copyright laws, it is not possible to insert the image of the sign. You can search for it on-line and/or use your imagination to see it in your mind's eye. It was a painting on a jewelry box she did in 2011.

Two Little Girls Come A Calling . . .

Yo, Yo, Yo, Yo,

One night, Mary had two little girls, Marie and Caelan, who wanted to come to our home. I think Mary said they were sisters. Oh, no, wait, they were cousins. I do not know what that word means but Mary used that word. They were so much fun. The littlest one, Caelan, chased me around for a little bit. She was so much fun. After awhile, she sat down on the settle and I climbed up to sit next to her. She was very, very kind and I wanted her to pet me. I snuggled her hand and she started petting me. Well, she laid her head on the pillow and fell asleep! I cuddled up next to her and went to sleep, too, under her arm. Mary put a blanket over us so we would be warm. It was heaven.

Now, the older girl, Marie, was most kind as well and she gave Mary a beautiful painting of a Black Footed Ferret. They are the Native American ferret and very wild. You see, we domestic ferrets are decedents of the European ferret. Just like the people who settled here in America. Well, Marie had just studied the Black Footed Ferrets in school and the painting was part of her assignment. She knew that Mary took care of us and wanted to give her the art. Mary was so grateful for the very personal gift. She laminated it and hung it on our Kondo, on the outside of the wall of the top floor. So we have two pieces of art, one from Stephanie, that Mary described in the past story, Now Tazz, and this new one. We are so fortunate and blessed . . . okay, now I want to tell you about the room I cannot get into in the next story.

The Gate

There is one room in our home that I cannot get into. It has been like that ever since I arrived. The people who built Mary's house, left a large gap under the bottom of the doors and between the floor. It is about two inches and means that I can go ANYWHERE I want Well, that meant I could go into Mary's office, too. She did not like us in that room because there was a lot of stuff that could hurt us if we got into it. So, Mary took a piece of plywood and propped it up so that we could not get past it or over it. She was pretty smart but she did not like the way it looked and set about to build the Gate.

She measured the door and it was 28 inches wide. She cut two pieces of 1" x 2" to 28 inches. Then she bought seven 1" x 3-1/2" x 42" French Gothic Fence Pickets and measured them out so that they would be equally spaced on the 1" x 2"s. Then she screwed them altogether on the back side so that they did not show on the front. After that, she cut a 1" x 4" for the diagonal part behind it, squared it up, and made sure it was all secured. Once it was all done, she painted it Jazz Purple. Her brother, Mike, installed it in the door frame for her so that it was about 1/4" off the floor. It is the prettiest gate you ever saw. She had always wanted a gate and Dutch door in her home. Now she had one of the two. And I had no way of getting into her office! We were safe to roam elsewhere around the house and that was just fine. But I really wish I could have spent time in that room. I bet there was a lot of fun to be had in there. Oh well, off to other adventures with Riley.

See ya, Tazz

In my own words

Note: The bags should be on the back side of the gate to prevent ferrets, like Racal, from climbing over it!

53

Well, hello there,

One Saturday, Mary took all of us to the vet. She found out that Rufia had a delicate heart condition and needed a lot of tender loving care. Well, she was in good hands as Mary was a good ferret mom. Sometime later, Rufia fell asleep one day and drifted off. It was the same thing that happened to my wife. When Mary got home, she took Rufia, wrapped her in a blanket and took her away. She was crying all the while as Rufia had passed away just like my LuLu. Rascal tried to get me to play but I was not interested in her. So, we maintained our distances and vied for Mary's attention. Good thing that Mary had two hands and a big heart so that she could pick us up and hold us together at the same time.

The summer of 2015 was a bit tough for me. Mary was in school on the weekends as she was getting her Permaculture Design Certificate. Not sure what that was but she was gone a lot and studied all of the time when she was home. She learned a lot about growing and caring for plants and animals in an urban homestead and on a small scale farm. She wanted to move her life from office jobs to being out in Mother Nature. While I did not have Insulinoma at the time, I did start to get a lot of mast cell tumors and needed to see the doctor a couple of times to have them removed. That was not too much of a problem until I developed a cough.

Mary took me to the vet straight away when she heard my cough. The vet gave her something called medicine for me to take. Let me tell you that the Ferretvite did NOT help the medicine go down. I do not care what Mary Poppins or Mary Dralle said about that. I did not like the medicine and put up a fuss. This went on for two weeks. When I did not get better, Mary took me back to see the what the vet would say.

Well, the vet took x-rays and found out that I had a really big heart. I could have told her that. Oh wait, she said I had an enlarged heart and would need different medicines for the rest of my days. Great, medicines, my least favorite food group!

TaTaForNow, Tazz

In my own words *Note*: Ferretvite was only used to help with the medicine. It is not a good food for ferrets to eat. Salmon oil is far better to help get them to sit still and take medicine . . . I found out about it recently while writing this book.

Ultimate Pet Fountain for my Health

Welcome back,

One day, in late March of 2016, Mary stayed home to take care of me. I had a couple of mast tumors removed without any sleepy-time drugs because of my big heart. I was grumpy and in a fair amount of pain. I got a bit upset with her as she did not hold me while I ate. I had gotten used to being pampered by her and did not kiss her for a couple of day even though she held me for every meal after that. After a couple of days, I needed a kiss from her and gave in! I am funny that way.

By Labor Day Weekend of 2016, I was slowing down a bit and while she was working around the house, Mary took a picture of me, Razz-Oh-My-Tazz, drinking from the Ultimate Pet Fountain . . . I really loved drinking from it!!! She made it in the spring time after reading about having good drinking water for me. Oh, and everyone else, too. She bought a two gallon stainless steel bowl and put it into an old tire so that I could not tip it over! She was so smart to do that. Then, she hooked up an Aquarium Water Filter, We had mostly clean water after that. I say mostly because Raven would drink water with his mouth full of cat food. Mary had to clean it out many times. In the summer of 2016, Mary's dad died and so did Raven. It was a hard time for her as they died within two weeks of each other. The good thing, the water was ALWAYS clean now.

My overall health was slowing down because of my big heart, well that, and I had developed advanced insulinoma. I was eating every hour or two to keep my strength up. Seeing me drink from the Ultimate Pet Fountain made Mary very happy as it kept me hydrated. I had not 'asked' her if I could leave as of that time, so she said that we would not be making a trip to see Dr. Cote anytime soon. Every time she came home, I was right there to greet her . . . and she never slept alone!!! I always wanted to be real close to her. She was such a blessing and I am so thankful that The Creator entrusted her to me . . .

From the bottom of my big heart,
Tazz

Tazz's Tribute, Sept 14, 2016

In my own words Well, this has been a week . . . a couple of months ago, Mr. Tazz, turned his nose up to any food that had his heart meds in it. Although I would put his pill into the goo, he would lick it all up and spit out the pill. So, I stopped giving him meds and I knew that his vet, Dr. Irene Cote, would not be happy. When I took Rascal in for her "Hormone" shot, I came clean to let her know how he was doing and that he was off his meds, his choice, not mine. She was not happy but understood that you can only force so hard before you just let them live as they want. For awhile, he was doing okay as long as he got his food on time, had lots of his Alkaline drinking water, his Lavender oil with Reiki, and to be swaddled with each nap.

I came home on Saturday to a little one who did not want food and I knew what was happening. The next couple of days were going to be very, very hard for all of us. Monday night, I came home from work to a little one who was sprawled on the hallway floor, shaking with cold and looking for me. I picked him up, carried him to the settle and swaddled him again. He refused food and I used a syringe to get the Alkaline water into him. I gave him his Lavender oil with Reiki and laid him on the settle next to me. I would gently touch him from time to time so that he knew I was still there for him. Later that night, I laid down to get some rest and put him next to me. About an hour later, I woke up and Tazz had moved. I picked him up and set him atop my right rib cage, a place he loved to sleep at night. Then I covered him with several layers of little blankets and then drifted back to sleep. At about 3 am, I heard this small voice say, 'Mom, I had a stroke', and woke up right away. He was paralyzed and his breathing had changed to that slow breath. And then, he drew his last breath and slipped away in my arms . . .

He is now at the Rainbow Bridge with his beloved LuLu . . . I am pretty sure that she was here to take him there.

After he was buried, his name was added to the Green Fleece WRI Memorial Jacket, Tazz . . . Always in my Heart. Daniel was kind enough to place it on the left side . . . Over my heart.

Mary

Her Acquaintance
Rascal - A Charcoal Sable Girl

Hello Friend,

After LuLu passed away, Mary thought it would be a good idea to get Tazz a friend. She was thinking about it when the phone rang out of the blue. There was a man who lived a couple of towns over and he was my daddy. Well, mine and Rufia's that is. She was my very best friend and we really had a good time at his house. He worked a lot and we had to stay in our cage most of the time. He had heard that Mary took in ferrets, from the man who gave her Tazz and LuLu, and decided to call her. She came over the very next day to meet us.

Rufia went down the stairs to the living room first. She was brave while I was a bit timid and shy. I watched Mary pick up Rufia and talk to her softly. She seemed a gentle person. She was talking to my daddy about the time we were taken away from him and the man who gave her Tazz and LuLu brought us back to him. Then they talked about what it was like to have ferrets in their homes and that Mary let hers roam all over all of the time. I decided to go downstairs and meet her.

Now, I had a special way of going down the stairs because I liked to hop down them. It was always so much fun to do it my way. Mary thought I was so cute that she met me at the bottom of the stairs and picked me up from the landing. She looked into my eyes and said, 'You really are a Rascal, aren't you!" She was very good hearted but she could not take us home that night because she was going out to Minnesota to visit her family. I am saying this because other people may need to delay taking in ferrets right away because of events in their lives!

As soon as she returned to California, she came right over and brought us to her home. We arrived and she set the carrier down on the living room floor. She opened the door and I stepped out. Tazz sniffed me and walked away. 'Good,' she said, as introduction was not a problem. BUT Tazz took one look at Rufia and attacked her.

Mary ran to help out Rufia and put Tazz in the Kriminal's Kondo to 'cool down'. Try as she might with gentle introductions, Tazz never really like Rufia. So, the decision was made to let Tazz out of the Kondo and we had to be in it or vice versa.

One night, Tazz was in the Kondo and had a hissy fit. Mary ran to see what was the matter and there were ants everywhere. She acted very quickly putting us into a carrier and letting him out of the Kondo. This had never happened before and she set to clean up everything. Once the Kondo was spotless, she put plates with baby powder on them under the wheels so that the ants could not crawl into the Kondo. Then she put him back in there and let us out of the carrier so that we could continue to play.

The next morning, she played a particular song from the Northern Cree and Friends Long Winter Nights CD called Mac No More. Tazz loved that song and could hardly wait to get out of the Kondo so he could dance with Mary. She would do a dance step and bounce him to the beat of the drum all around the island in the kitchen. She would move clockwise just like she did at powpows. He loved it.

After sometime, Tazz would tolerate being in the same room as us but he would not play at all. At least, we were all allowed out of the Kondo and could come and go in it as we pleased. Most of the time, Rufia and I would sprint up to the penthouse. That was not Tazz's favorite place as he loved the inside of Mary's closet. Northeast corner to be exact, under her tops on the faux lamb's wool cover left over from Mary's knee replacement surgeries.

Now I have gone a great deal about others but I have not shared much about myself. I am a charcoal sable. Means I am very dark gray with a pretty little mask on my face. I am rather petite as far as ferrets go and I walk very delicately and quietly. I will look for Mary where ever she may be in our home and look into her eyes, bat my big eye lashes as to say, Escuse me (I do not pronounce 'X' s very well 'cuz I have a lisp). I love to be held and cuddled. It is my very favorite.

When Rufia and I were out and about, we slept in one of three places: atop the Krminal's Kondo in the Penthouse, behind the 'fireplace' or under the bookcase!

58

We love scampering in and out of our tubes on the floor and climbing/sliding in the one around the Krminal's Kondo to the Penthouse. We can play for about two hours on a good morning. Then we have a bite to eat and take a nap!

Bye for now,
Rascal

In my own words In February of 2017, Rascal, aka Lil Miss Escuse Me, had gone on to meet Rufia at the Rainbow Bridge. It was the first time since January, 2011, that our home did not have little furry ones. She is dearly missed to this day and I am glad that I had the chance to tell her to run to Rufia if she saw her before she drew her last breath. She was so loved.

In the days that followed, she was added to my green fleece WRI jacket as Lil' Miss Escuse Me.

Her Acquaintance

Rufia – A Dark Eyed White

Hello Friend,

I am the second ferret in this partnership with Rascal. I love life and am a very genteel ferret with manners. I eat a little bit at a time, do not chase after cats like some ferrets do, and always used the designated litter box! A very proper lady indeed.

I liked Mary from the start as she had a very gentle voice. She can raise it if required but that does not happen too much in our day to day living. And we do like to live. Rascal and I take turns with Tazz being out of the Kriminal's Kondo. When we are in the Kondo, we have fun playing with all of the toys and blankets. When we are out and about, our favorite pastime is tube chasing! Especially when we get to climb up the Penthouse Access Tube and slide down on our tummies. One time we did it about 20 times. It was so much fun. My favorite place to sleep is in the round bed atop the Penthouse.

The next best thing is cuddle time. Rascal and I are inseparable for the most part. When I am hungry, I go find Mary and try to climb up her leg so I can whisper in her ear and ask for food. She gives us a lot of different foods to eat. My favorite is chicken baby food, Beechnut, to be specific! And I do like their turkey as well. Also, I like to sneak the cat's kibble when they are not looking.

Neither Rascal not I participate in shenanigans like other ferrets. Rascal has a cute charming personality and she displays it often. But neither of us steal stuff and hide it. That is not how a ferret with manners behaves.

Now, Mary would take all of us to see the nice woman. She would feel us and let Mary know that we were okay. One time, she listened to my heart beat with the cold round shinny thing and told Mary that something did not sound right.

61

She took me back to a different part of her place, put a lot of those cold round shinny things on me. After a bit, she told my Mary she thought something was off with my heart and asked if she could take a picture of it. Mary did not sound happy when she said yes.

Well, the nice woman found out I had a heart condition and that I needed a special liquid two times a day. Mary was pretty quite on the drive home. When we got there, Rascal and I started our playtime together and life was fun 'scept when I had to drink that liquid. It tasted terrible and I did not like it at all.

Days turned into weeks and then months. One night, when Rascal and I were sleeping in the Kondo, I felt drawn to this beautiful place. I will describe it to you ... There were meadows and hills where I could run and play together with my litter mates ...there was plenty of food, water and sunshine so that I was warm and comfortable ... I felt restored to health and vigor all the while being whole and strong again ... It was a great place for me to be and I said goodbye to Rascal. In the morning, Mary thought it was strange that Rascal was not sleeping on me. When she felt my lifeless body, she let out a big sigh and tears rolled down her face. A couple of days after she buried me, my name was place on her green fleece WRI jacket that read, Precious Rufia, on a special place close to her heart.

Lovingly,

Rufia

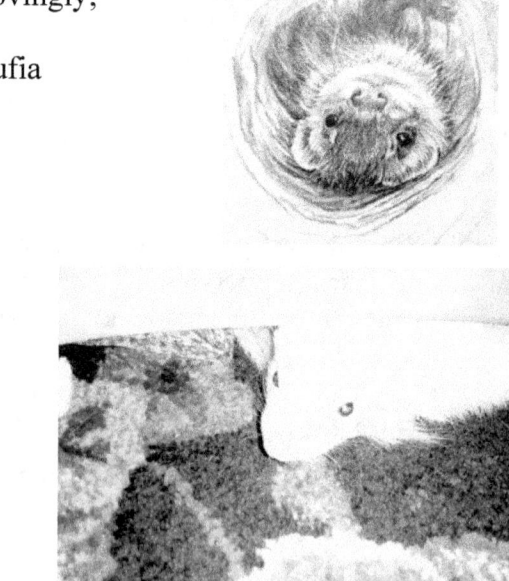

Her Acquaintance

Bonnie – A Chocolate Sable

In my own words In September of 2018, I brought Bonnie and Dylan home to live  with us. Bonnie had a rough life. She and her first husband, Clyde, were abandoned and found eating out of a trash dumpster. Try as she might, their previous owner had a hard time keeping them healthy. Clyde succumbed to an intestinal obstruction that took his life and Bonnie was left alone. The wonderful owner brought in two more Kriminals, Dillinger and his friend. Unfortunately, the friend passed away. Thus, Bonnie and Dylan (name changed because he was so very calm and peaceful for a boy who was not a rough tough Dillinger type!) joined our happy home. This is her story.

Hello Friend,

This house is wonderful and our Kondo is great, too. Our former owner wanted Mary to have our other cage but May did not know how to get it into her home or where she was going to put it because she already had one. She told our other owner to sell it as she was a bit strapped for funds. Now, we have four levels in this cage and appreciate the very top level most of all. My poor second husband does have a tough time falling off the top and Mary was good about getting the bumpers installed so that no longer happens. What a wonderful woman she is about our constant care.

What we love the best is being able to go anywhere we want, anytime we want. It is wonderful. We had a lot of fun exploring this new home. I found an old dryer vent tube in the corner of the laundry one evening and was able to make a sizeable hole in it. Once I got through the hole, I pushed on the plastic door and punched it out. Next thing I knew, I was outside in the wide, wide world and there was a lot to explore! I went up the front steps and when Rachel, the calico cat, spotted me outside, she called for Riley and they let Mary know where I was.

Mary was not too happy and came outside right away but I started to giggle and ran as fast as I could across the deck and around the side of the house. I kept running over the patio and up the back slope. Mary stopped chasing me and I crossed the street to the neighbor's yard. It was full of hard rocks and then I saw Mary's van pull up. She spotted me right away and before I could start running, she picked me up, we got into van and she drove us back home.

When we got home, she locked both of us in our Kondo and we heard a lot of banging and such. Later, she opened the door and we hopped out. I ran to the laundry room and the tube was gone. In its place was a big piece of plywood. My hole was blocked and I had to stay in the house with my second husband and the cats. Bummer because I love being outside . . .

My First Little Boo-boo

Our previous owner told Mary that I had a problem with getting infections. My health is not that great after living with Clyde in the dumpster. We did the best we could with what we had in the time allotted but it was a very dirty life and I got sick, a lot. One Saturday night, I went to sleep and felt just fine. I am going to let Mary tell this story because of her boy, Tazz. He checked in on me and said he would tell Mary there was a little problem.

Bye for now,
Bonnie

In my own words *This is how I, Mary, saw events play out that weekend .*On the Saturday night of the last weekend in October of 2018, there was an interesting event. My grandma, Helen Dralle*, was trying to tell me something but I could not hear clearly. It had to do with three water bottles I was about to drain out. I heard her say, save those, you are going to need them. I woke up on Sunday morning to no water! I used that saved water to rinse off my hands after I washed them.

Note: For many of us of Celtic/Germanic decent, we understand the true meaning of Halloween or Samhain (pronounced **saa**·wn) is a time when the veil between the two worlds is very thin. For me, I hear my ancestors, like my grandma and dad, guiding me in this lifetime on a regular basis.

During the night, in my sleep, Tazz popped in to my dreams three times. He was trying to tell me about Bonnie. When I had fed her Saturday night dinner, she was fine. Little did I know that she would wake up with a big boo-boo. She had a huge bump on her forehead. It was such a blessing to find out that there was a ferret vet, Doc Martin, I kid you not, the next city over who was willing to take a look at her and help out on Sunday morning. She had surgery that day to clear up the encapsulated abscess and I asked for prayers from the Ferrets For Life Facebook group. When I picked her up that night, I came in singing, 'My Bonnie Lies over the Ocean', but the lab tech did not appreciate me that much. I said, 'Thank you Universe and Tazz.'

At 7:34 that Sunday night, we still did not have water. It was a good thing I had saved the water and made extra for dinner the night before!!! Thank you Universe and Grandma for your guidance.

By Halloween, Riley the cat's birthday, Miss Bonnie was back in business and up to her usual shenanigans. She had to stay in her Kriminal Kondo and on that night, it was opened and she was free to move about the domicile. She ate her raw chicken, I checked her boo-boo and she is sleeping in her favorite hammock. She healed up marvelously thanks to all of the prayers and love that came in from our Ferrets for Life group. All I could say was, THANK YOU SO MUCH FROM THE BOTTOM OF BOTH OF OUR HEARTS!!!

Bonnie's Second Little Boo-boo

Life was going along fine until one Sunday morning seven months later. You know it is going to be a tough Mother's Day in 2019 when you wake up to Bonnie with a bloody eye. I was not sure if it was spousal abuse from Dylan or one of the cats but Little Bonnie has another boo-boo. I took her back over to the same vet and it was really bad news as she had to have her eye removed the next morning. Once again, I had asked that the Ferrets for Life group would send her love and light for a successful surgery and speedy recovery. Come to find out, another serious infection had pushed her eye out of its socket. It was a great comfort to know that she did not lose her eye because of Dylan or the cats. She came home that Monday night to her favorite bed, raw chicken thighs and her hubby whom she slept with all night long. She took her medicine the next morning without a fuss. She healed up well and was back to her shenanigans within one week's time.

Again, life was so wonderful for the next year and a half. I was very lucky that these ferrets were on the raw food diet. It really is the best way to feed them and keep them healthy. Both Bonnie and Dylan were dainty eaters. Not once did they hork down their food like it was their last meal! They were so much fun to play with, watch and take care of. Even if Dylan did not like to use the privy the way he should have. That ferret never did get the hang of litter training and we just had pee pads on all but the top level of the Kondo. Life was so very good.

One Thursday night in mid-March of 2020, I came home to find Bonnie lying on my bed is a terrible state. While she was fine in the morning before I left for work, she had another infection set in during the day. All of the vets were closed for the evening. During the night, she slept with me so that I could take care of her and, then, at some point, she passed away without a good bye. After she was buried, and the words, 'Beautiful Bonnie' were added to my Green Fleece WRI Memorial Jacket.

Of all of my ferrets, she was the smartest and cleverest. I miss her asking me to pick her up so that she could kiss me.

Mary

Her Acquaintance
Dylan – A Dark Eyed White

Hi There,

With me, there is not a whole lot of my story that is outside of what Bonnie shared. Like she said, I was her second husband and my personality is a bit laid back. I did not want to play with the cats at all. I mean, I liked them but I would much rather be anywhere with Bonnie. Especially in the penthouse.

Keeping cool in summer heat - Dylan's story, too

I will share this: I had a very hard time with the hot summer months and Mary took very good care of me. Here is what she did. She had 'ferret' plates in the freezer and lots of 'ferret' water bottles, too. Every four to six hours, she would take out a plate and two water bottles and place them in our round bed in the penthouse. The water bottles were wrapped up in ferret wash cloths and set on top of the plate at 45 degrees. The \ / that Tazz described. I would put one armpit on one bottle and the other armpit on the second one. Then I would rest my head where they met while my belly and back were on the bottle's sides. Also, I had my own personal fan. The only time that Mary used all of those items was for me. Well, she did part of them for Tazz, too. She was very good about cleaning and sanitizing them BEFORE putting them back into the freezer. She had said it was the way her Mom had raised her. I guess that woman really loved bleach. Thankfully, Mary bought a Hypochlorous Acid (HOCl) generator and made it fresh all of the time. She used it to clean our cages as well. She said it was better than bleach because it is non-toxic and can be made from a simple salt water solution. Now, I am just a ferret and listened to Mary explain it to me. When she was in school, she studied Chemistry. After awhile, it put me to sleep . . .

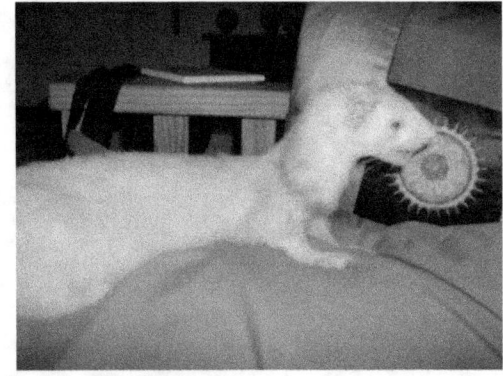

Good night, Friend, Dylan

In my own words *Mary here again.* Life with Dylan was good. After Bonnie passed, I did not get him anyone else as he did not seem to want anyone but me or his penthouse bed. I would cuddle him from the time I got home from work until I went to sleep at night. Often times, he would crawl into my bed and sleep with me.

The week of Thanksgiving 2020 came. He seemed fine right up until the end. On Tuesday night of that week, he passed away without saying good bye just like Bonnie. And I did not hear her come to get him either. I know that they are at Rainbow Bridge with each other and their friends. Shortly after his passing and burial, and the words, 'Dylan Darling' were added to my Green Fleece WRI Memorial Jacket.

An aside . . .

As of the printing of this book, I have not had ferrets since Dylan's passing. I long for the day when I can have a couple more and hear the pitter patter of their shenanigans in my home. Ferrets really are God's little pranksters who are so full of life and joy. If you want to see what I mean, check out Youtube for the video, 'Are FERRETS FUNNIER than CATS & DOGS? See for yourself!' by Tiger Productions.

My Green Fleece WRI Memorial Jacket

On the left,
In Loving Memory of Milady D'Ferret ? - 5/12/12
(The '?' is used because I did not know when she was born)

In Loving Memory of Mundungus Ferret

LuLu La Ferret You were loved

Dylan Darling

On the right

In Memory of Dave Bittner

Precious Rufia

Tazz Always in my Heart

Lil Miss Escuse Me

Beautiful Bonnie

69

Some Ferret Related Odds and Ends

Many of the following pages are of unknown origin/authors and useful just the same

The Sprite and the Stone . . .
by Mary 'Klibs' Dralle

Dear Friend,

Sometimes, little girl ferrets like me are called sprites, because we cannot have babies.

Here is a story of a Sprite and the Stone . . .

Once upon a time there was a hob, a beautiful sable male ferret, looking for a jill, a female ferret. He looked all throughout the forest, up the trees and in all of the tunnels trying to find the jill of his dreams. He could not find anyone to share his burrow. One very rainy night, he returned to his burrow tired and exhausted after his search with a bit of sad heart because he could not find a friend. You see, ferrets like to have a lot of friends around them, called a business, and do not like to be alone. The little hob curled up in a blanket that he found on a trail one time and went to sleep.

Meanwhile, there was a small white sprite wandering the forest trying to find a warm, dry place to sleep. She was very cold from the rain and did not watch where she was going when she fell down a hole. She realized that there was no more rain falling on her and was happy. As she moved down the tunnel, she came across a blanket. She breathed a sigh of relief and tugged it over herself to sleep. Try as she might to fall asleep, she could not as there was a small jagged stone that kept poking her. She would get up, tug the blanket some more and try to curl up to sleep but still the stone poked her and she could not sleep. She was becoming very upset and finally fell asleep because of exhaustion.

Now, while our little sprite was tugging and pulling on the blanket, the little hob, whose hole she had fallen into, was sleeping through the night. He was having a dream that a beautiful, white ferret was tucking him in so that he could sleep better. When she was done with his blankets, she would lay down next to him. Every now and again, he would have the dream over and over again. This was his heart's true desire, to have someone who would share his castle with and be near him.

After some time and the rain had passed, the hob woke up and stretched. He crawled out from under his blanket and went out into the forest to look for food and a ferret to keep him company. After eating a small vole, he returned to his hole. He could not believe his eyes. There was a small white sprite asleep on his blanket and she looked just like the ferret in his dream.

He went over and smelled her and woke her up. She was frightened and started to fight with him. The hob did not know what to do. She was so pretty. He did not fight back and then the little sprite noticed that he was not fighting with her and stopped. She was in a bit of pain because she had slept on that stone and was not thinking straight. The little hob gently touched her nose with his. The little sprite touched him back. Then the little hob left his hole. He thought that she might be hungry like he got when he woke up and went to find her something to eat. The little sprite was confused and laid back on top of the blanket.

Awhile later, the hob returned with a meal for the sprite. She gobbled down the mouse and was so happy; she did the weasel dance in the hob's hole. The hob was happy that the little sprite was joy filled. He squealed at her but she said nothing and kept dancing. He chirped but the sprite said nothing and kept dancing. There was a loud crash outside the hole that scared the hob but the sprite just kept dancing around the hole. The little hob had heard that some ferrets were deaf but had never met one. Here was this beautiful white sprite in his home and he realized that she was deaf.

After the sprite finished celebrating her new friend, she stopped dancing. She had a hard time making friends because she was deaf. She had longed to find someone who would take care of her and be a true friend. She looked at the hob and then touched his nose. He was scared; how would he talk to her? He touched her nose again and she started to dance again. He started to dance with her. It was a fun game and the little hob realized that he did not have to say anything to get her to dance. Then she turned on him and tickled him . . . he laughed and laughed. He was happy with the little sprite. After awhile, they were both tired. He crawled into his blanket and so did she. She pulled the blanket all around them and snuggled next to the hob. He realized his dream had come true and he found the sprite of his dream . . . they lived in the hole in the forest floor for many years. They went hunting together every day, frolicked on the banks of the stream in the summer, and took long naps together in their blanket. They lived happily ever after . . . The End

Ferrets genders names

A male ferret is called a hob.
A female ferret is called a jill,
A baby ferret is called a kit.
Also, when you spay a female ferret she is called a sprite.
A de-sexed male is called a gib.
A vasectomised male is called a hoblet.
And a group of ferrets is known as a "business" because they are busy!
The get into all kinds of mischief and shenanigans!

Some Myths About Ferrets . . .

Myth Number 1 ~ *Ferrets are wild animals*. While we do have cousins that are wild ferrets, such as he black footed ferret, we domestic ferrets have been domestic for thousands of years and are thought to be a domesticated Western or Eastern European polecat. The Eastern European or Steppe polecat (Mustela eversmanni) and the Eastern European polecat (Mustela putorius putorius) are very similar in appearance and skeletal structure. We ferrets can interbreed and produce fertile offspring with either of these species of polecat.

Myth Number 2 ~ *Domestic ferrets are dangerous pets*. We domestic ferrets are often classified as exotic pets. And some people lump tigers, lions, alligators, and alike, as exotic pets. In reality, they are not exotic just less common than cats and dogs

Myth Number 3 ~ *Ferrets stink*. Well, yes we can. Any animal kept in a dirty cage is going to stink. The trick is to keep their cage and bedding clean. This actually works to my advantage.

Myth Number 4 ~ *Ferrets are nocturnal animals*. One neat thing about us is our schedule will match yours, sort of. We usually get up at dawn for a couple hours, take a long nap, and up in the late afternoon into the evening. This is a similar pattern to ferrets and weasels in nature. You see, we do not do well with the heat of the day and will stay in our cool burrows instead.

Myth Number 5 ~ *Ferrets are prolific breeders*. Actually, we ferrets have an unusual husbandry. Both hobs (males) and jills (females) have to be in season. If we jills enter estrus and are not bred, we will die. An intact male ferret will smell so bad that few people would want them in the house. So, there is very little 'backyard' breeding of ferrets. Most come from large breeders and are already spayed or neutered when they are sold at the pet store. That is why we have tattoos in our ears

Myth Number 6 ~ *Ferrets are rodents*. This is the most offensive statement to us Ferrets. We are NOT rodents but mustelids. Our family includes otters, badgers, weasels, martens, minks, polecats, stoats, and wolverines, to name a few. We ferrets are the only domesticated members of this family.

The Ten Commandments for a Responsible Ferret Parent (Farent)

Based on Paul Harvey's "10 Commandments for a Responsible Pet Owner"

1. My life is likely to last 5-8 years. Any separation from you will be painful. When you decide to make me part of your life, let it be forever. If at some time in our lives you cannot keep me, make sure that my new home will provide what I need and will supply the love, care and socialization I crave.

2. Let me teach you to understand me and what I need from you. I will test you from time to time to make sure you remember the lessons.

3. Keep me safe and secure. Protect me from others that would harm me. I depend on you. You are my lifeline.

4. Talk to me and cuddle me. Your voice is as enjoyable to my ears as birds sweetly singing are to yours. Your gentle touch is as warm as the soft rays of the sun.

5. I need fresh nutritious raw meat and fresh water, warm clean blankets to cuddle in during winter, and cool clean sheets with a frozen water bottle to lay on in the heat of the summer. My litter box and cage should be cleaned daily. Hugs and social time each and every day. Do not put me in a cage outside. I belong inside with my family.

6. I will make many mistakes. I am not perfect. Be gentle when you correct.

7. Don't get angry at me. I am an intelligent, joyous, curious creature and WILL get into things. Know that this is how I am. I am not trying to be destructive. I depend on you to watch out for me and protect me from danger.

8. Never hit me or shake me. I am small and can be hurt very easily. When you are angry at someone or something else, do not take it out on me. I have nothing to give you but love and joy. This is my true nature.

9. Take special care of me as I grow older. I may play less but I still love you just as much as when I was young enough to dance. Monitor me closely for I will experience ailments as I grow older.

10. When I can no longer enjoy life and am in pain with no relief, please stay with me till the end. I have given you my life and my love. Don't disappoint me in my last moments here on this earth. Tell me that you love me and hold me close. Let my passing be gentle. Always remember that I love you.

Other names for ferrets:

Woozel

Squeezils

Carpet Shark

Toe Shark

Weasel

Sock puppets

Little bandits

Dookers

Dancing Dookers

Stinkminks

And a great many more

Well Known Ferret Property Laws

1. If I like it, it's mine.

2. If it's in my mouth, it's mine.

3. If I had it a little while ago, it's mine.

4. If I can take it from you, it's mine.

5. If it looks like mine, it's mine.

6. If it's mine, it must never be yours.

7. If I saw it first, it's mine.

8. If you have something and put it down, it's mine.

9. If I chew something up, all of the pieces are mine.

10. If it used to be yours, get over it.

11. If it's edible, it's always mine.

12. If it's broken, it's yours.

~Unknown

MLD

My Recipe for Duck Soup

Sometimes, when domestic Ferrets feel under the weather, they like to have a wee bit of Duck Soup. Mind you, it doesn't have duck in it but was named after a weasel named Duck. He ate it and got all better! This is my version of the soup . . . I am a vegetarian and cutting up the raw meat for my wee ones, well, just one word, yuck!

INGREDIENTS

3 cups water

1 chicken thigh, bone in, skinned

2 egg yolks, whisked in a bowl and set aside

Place water into saucepan and bring to boil on stove.

Add the chicken thigh and simmer, uncovered, for 30-40 minutes or until meat falls off the bone

Remove meat and bone from the broth and set aside to cool down a bit. Cut into small ferret bite sized pieces.

Meanwhile, add the raw egg yolks to the broth and stir continuously until they are cooked through.

Remove pan from stove and add the cut up chicken back into the broth.

Allow soup to cool before feeding ferret.

Other foods used to keep ferrets healthy

On occasion, if you think your ferret needs to have an emergency moving experience, you can give them a bit of canned pumpkin. This is only done if you think they have eaten something that they should have left alone and should not be given very often.

Salmon oil, on the other hand, can be given as a daily treat. Many of us will put a dab on their stomachs so that we can administer a four paw pedicure! It is just wonderful to have on hand.

I Heard Your Voice In The Wind Today
Author Unknown

I heard your voice in the wind today,
and turned to see your face.
the warmth of the wind caressed me,
as I stood silently in place.

I felt your touch in the sun today,
as its warmth filled the sky.
I closed my eyes for your embrace,
and my spirit soared high.

I saw your eyes in the window pane,
as I watched the falling rain.
It seemed as each raindrop fell,
it quietly said your name.

I held you close in my heart today,
it made me feel complete.
You may have died... but you are not gone,
you will always be a part of me.

As long as the sun shines,
the wind blows,
the rain falls.
You will always live on inside of me forever,
for that is all my heart knows.

This poem is often shared on many of the social media pages
when a ferret passes on and we still feel them near.

The Plan

Every now and again, my friend, Euel Oliver, will post this into a couple of the Ferret Groups on Facebook. He did not know who wrote it and has given me permission to share it here, in this book, as this is the story of my ferrets as well . . .

Once upon a time, in the Before time . . .

Wait a minute you say, that's not how stories start! What's the "before time"? Well the Before time is the time and place before our Mortal existence where we gathered all our loved ones together and mapped out our lives in this world.

Once upon a time, in the Before time . . . a little spirit of the four legged kind called her loved ones together. She said to them, "this is my plan: I wish to be a Ferret. Ferrets are happy creatures. They bounce, they run, they play, they bring laughter and happiness to the world. Ferrets know true joy and know to share it. That would seem to be a good life and one with purpose. It will be mine and I will serve in this way.

For the first half of my life, I wish to know the emptiness of neglect so that in the second half of my life when I come to know love I will recognize it for what it is. I wish for my life to be difficult, to know pain and illness for through these challenges we become stronger, more perfect beings. I wish to know the confines of bars and cages, then to learn the joy of open air and sunlight. I wish to live in darkness so that I may hear, see and taste the goodness of the world. But I do not wish to endure these things alone" as she looked around at her loved ones gathered there. They all knew her road would be harder than most but the rewards would be greater and admired her for her wisdom and courage.

Then she looked to the girl spirit, one of the two legged variety, whom she had summoned to her gathering. "Of you I have a special request. When it is time, I wish to die in a place where the grass is green and streams sing gentle songs and the trees whisper. Where the earth is clean, the flowers sweet and the air pure, that I may feel once again as one with the Creator.

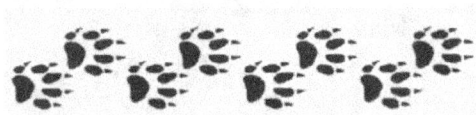

I wish you to teach me of these things, for they will become the essence of my personality and being. Then I wish you to return me Home, my journey completed."

The girl hung her head in sadness for she loved all things wrought by the Creator deeply. "You ask much of me little soul, and I fear I will not be able to do as you ask. I fear the pain and guilt would be too much and would haunt me for all of my days upon the Earth, yet I do not wish to deny you your chosen path."

The little soul, who had already acquired the form of a ferret, stepped into the girl's lap and looked up into her eyes. "Then we will make a bargain you and I." She once again looked about the circle of loved ones around her and made this promise: "I will bring to you my brothers and sisters of the four legged kind. I will bring to the chosen day a sister of your kind. They will share the pain you will feel and in doing so, ease that burden." A tear welled in the eye of the girl for it was not her nature to stand in the way of another's chosen fate, yet she knew that this would break her mortal heart. She feared her strength would fail her on the chosen day.

Once again the little spirit looked into her eyes and seeing the pain there offered more. "Still I see this is too great a burden for you, so I offer you this: Return me to a place you and I will choose now, and I will go alone, thus freeing you from this difficult task." The girl's eyes widened in horror. "Surely you know if I abandon you it would be worse! Do you not see that this would torment me through the rest of my mortal existence? Never knowing what had become of you would be an unhealed wound. This I cannot do."

The little soul looked into her eyes again and this time with greater compassion. "I will bring sisters and brothers of both kinds to share your pain and so lessen it. I will choose when and go alone as I see now I must. Any other way is asking too much. I will leave for you a sign, proof that I have returned Home as is my Plan. In that way you will be spared. Afterwards, I will stay with you until the grief has eased, the guilt is gone, and you can once more remember there was a Plan, my plan, a plan of my own choosing."

The girl looked up, one tear still upon her cheek. "It is still much you ask of me. This will bring pain to others as well as me. You are dear to me and I see you are determined and it is, after all,
your Plan.

I do not do this gladly, but for you I will suffer it." And with the agreement made, a bargain struck, the lights of their two souls blended and brightened, each giving to the other.

Once upon a time . . . In the spring when everything is green, sweet, when the streams sing their gentle songs and the trees whisper, a little blind ferret named Soda tread the last part of her journey alone and saw her plan fulfilled. She kept her bargain with the girl. She returned home but left the promised sign, the empty shell of her mortal body, to prove she had found her way. As promised her brothers and sisters where there to ease the pain, and also as promised so was the girl's sister. Plan fulfilled, bargain kept, she's Home.

We love you little Soda.

Credit to whoever wrote this

Keeping your Ferret(s) Out of the Couch

As mentioned, I belong to several Ferret Facebook pages, up to and including, Ferrets For Life. We share a lot in that group and it is how I have met some of the calibrators for this book. One such person is Quinten York, who had this brilliant idea for his couch. He used a vinyl lattice fence panel to make it ferret proof on the bottom. Wooden block in the corners add security and up to the publishing date of this book, they are not able to get into it. I love this idea even though I do not have a couch!

Ferrets At Work

A couple of days before April Fool's Day, 2022, the Iowa State University Police Department announced that they where switching from drug sniffing dogs to drug sniffing ferrets. Well, ferrets do have a very good sense of smell and we were all excited about the news. On 4/1/22, they had an updated post saying it was just a joke for April Fool's, or is that fools.

Be that as it may, ferrets are used for work and here are a couple of examples:

Misty was the ferret who ran cables at Buckingham Palace for the wedding of Princess Diana and Prince Charles in 1981.

A team of ferrets named Beckham, Posh, and Baby laid the TV, lighting, and sound cables under the stage for the millennium concert in Greenwich Park.

The 1st Battalion of the Yorkshire Regiment were presented with two ferrets when they were on duty in Northern Ireland. Ultimately, they were adopted as regimental pets and named after the battalion's battle honors, Imphal and Quebec. These ferrets are classified as regimental pets since they are not recognized by the Army.

And, let's not forget all of the ferrets used by European farmers to keep the rodent population out of their crops. After all, that is where the expression, 'ferreting out a hole' came from!

WTF
Where's the Ferret

A Howler from Euel ...

Dear Ferrets
When I say to move, it means go someplace else, not switch positions with each other so there are still two ferrets in the way.

The dishes with the paw print are yours and contain your food. The other dishes are mine and contain my food. Please note, placing a paw print in the middle of my plate of food does not stake a claim for it becoming your food and dish, nor do I find that aesthetically pleasing in the slightest.

The stairway was not designed by NASCAR and is not a racetrack. Beating me to the bottom is not the object. Tripping me doesn't help, because I fall faster than you can run.

I cannot buy anything bigger than a king size bed. I am very sorry about this. Do not think I will continue to sleep on the couch to ensure your comfort. Look at videos of ferrets sleeping, they can actually curl up in a ball. It is not necessary to sleep perpendicular to each other stretched out to the fullest extent possible. I also know that sticking tails straight out and having tongues hanging out the other end to maximize space used is nothing but ferret sarcasm.

My compact discs are not miniature Frisbees.

For the last time, there is not a secret exit from the bathroom. If by some miracle I beat you there and manage to get the door shut, it is not necessary to claw, whine, try to turn the knob, or get your paw under the edge and try to pull the door open. I must exit through the same door I entered. In addition, I have been using bathrooms for years, ferret attendance is not mandatory.

The proper order is kiss me, then go smell the other ferrets butt.
I cannot stress this enough.
It would be such a simple change for you.

Written by Euel Oliver
For Nyxa Lakeroad
Ferret Farm Rescue Shelter
May 30, 2005

You are more than my
FERRET . . .
You are a Reminder
from the Creator about
Precious Life . . .
You are my Happiness
when you are Silly . . .
You are my Joy when I
am Sad . . .
You are my Solace
when I am Weary . . .
You are my Best Friend
and I Love You

You are more than just
a Human . . .
You have rescued me
from harm . . .
You care for me with
food, a home, and love
You delight in my
shenanigans and your
smile melts my heart . . .
You are my Best Friend
and I Love You

Inspired by You are more than series of animal art
prints who's authorship is unknown
Mary Dralle, March 2022, Creator

89

A smile changes everything . . . .

About the author . . .

Mary 'Klibs' Dralle went to school for chemistry as it relates to the environment. As environmental jobs in the area were hard to come by at the time, she became a quality control chemist for local laboratories. Eventually, she moved from chemistry into Manufacturing as a Technical Writer
All of her working life, she volunteered for a variety of nature based organizations and her Church. In the 1990's she started to study permaculture. She has a great respect for Our Mother, The Earth, and man's impact on the environment. She became a certified Permaculture Designer in 2015 and is a marvelous chef. She loves to help people go Farm-To-Table in their own yards. On the third Saturday of the month, she works at a local farmer's market as the Resident Chef creating dishes on the spot with ingredients from the farmers and vendors.
Mary loving welcomes those little ones in need of a new home where they can revel in all of the possibilities.

to contact Mary 'Klibs' Dralle,
about ferrets, permaculture,
cooking or labyrinths,
please email her at
dancing.raven_rrc@yahoo.com

thank you so much for reading
this book to the very end